QUIZEROO

john huehnergarth

QUIZZES, TRICKS, STUNTS, PUZZLES, AND BRAIN TEASERS FROM TELL ME WHY

BY ARKADY LEOKUM

GROSSET & DUNLAP · Publishers · NEW YORK

1978 PRINTING

Library of Congress Catalog Card Number: 73-5373

ISBN: 0-448-11536-5 (Trade Edition)
ISBN: 0-448-03905-2 (Library Edition)

The contents of this book were previously published under
the titles *The Quiz Book* and *Puzzles, Stunts, Brain Teasers
and Tricks from "Tell Me Why."*

Contents

IT'S A SNAP

Blindfold a friend and snap your fingers near his right ear. He'll guess the direction the sound comes from. Now snap your fingers near his left ear. He'll guess correctly again. Now snap your fingers beneath his chin. He'll be completely fooled!

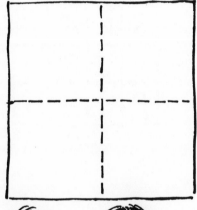

A QUARTER BET

Try this at a party, just for fun. Give someone a square piece of paper and say, "If you can tear this into four equal pieces, I'll give you a quarter." Naturally, he'll be able to do it. Then just give him one of the four pieces!

NOT IN

Try this on a friend — but make him answer quickly. Ask him to tell you the opposite of "Not in." He's almost sure to say, "Out." But the opposite of "Not in" is "In!"

HOW MANY?

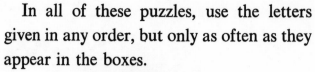

In all of these puzzles, use the letters given in any order, but only as often as they appear in the boxes.

How many words about CLOTHING can you make from the letters in these boxes? See if you can form at least fifteen of them.

I	F	K	C
S	N	T	V
A	J	R	E
P	U	H	O

How many words about INSECTS can you make from the letters in these boxes? See if you can form at least ten of them.

O	I	M	G
N	C	S	L
F	P	T	Y
H	E	W	A

How many words about EATING can you make from the letters in these boxes? See if you can form at least ten of them.

B	P	I	F
N	O	C	U
S	W	R	D
A	E	H	T

Answers at back of the book.

How many words about THE CIRCUS can you make from the letters in these boxes? See if you can form at least ten of them.

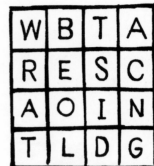

W	B	T	A
R	E	S	C
A	O	I	N
T	L	D	G

E	F	R	O
C	O	G	A
D	T	W	S
H	X	N	L

How many words about FARM ANIMALS can you make from the letters in these boxes? See if you can form at least ten of them.

W	L	G	R
S	E	H	C
I	O	K	A
T	B	N	G

How many words about BIRDS can you make from the letters in these boxes? See if you can form at least ten of them.

Answers at back of the book.

FIRE FOOLERS

This trick will fool your friends. Challenge one of them to light a match under water. Of course, he can't do it.

The trick is to fill a glass with water and hold it up. Then light a match under it!

Get an ordinary kitchen funnel and blow into it while holding a lighted match opposite the center of the funnel. Your breath will blow the flame TOWARD you!

The reason this happens is that your breath creates a partial vacuum at the center, whereupon the atmosphere pushes air into this vacuum and blows the flame toward you.

Line up three small cans on a table. Hold your mouth about two inches in front of the first can and a lighted match about two inches behind the last can. When you blow, you will be able to blow out the match!

The reason this happens is that your stream of air will divide when it strikes the cans. Each half of this stream is held against the sides of the cans by atmospheric pressure. Then the halves unite and blow out the flame.

WATER FOOLERS

Announce to your friends that you can hold your hand over a cup of water and get it wet without touching either the cup or the water. And you can do it!

The trick is to pour steaming water into the cup. When you hold your hand over it, it will become wet.

This trick is just for laughs. Tell your friend, "I bet I can stay under water for a whole minute." When he challenges you, just fill a glass with water and hold it over your head!

Fill a glass with water and place a coin behind it, as shown. Now try to look at the coin through the top of the glass so that you see it through the water and the other side of the glass. But you won't be able to see it!

CHANGE THE WORD

In all of these puzzles, see if you can change the first word to the end one in just four moves. Change one letter in the word with each move. (For example, you could change POUR into FAIL as follows: POUR, FOUR, FOUL, FOIL, FAIL.) Use the boxes, writing in the words from top to bottom.

Answers will be found at the back of the book.

STAR ... FEET

SNOW ... FLAG

THE PUZZLING PIE

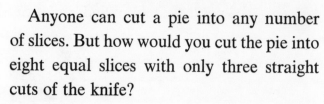

Anyone can cut a pie into any number of slices. But how would you cut the pie into eight equal slices with only three straight cuts of the knife?

Cut the pie into four quarters, pile these on top of one another, and make a single cut through the center!

THE PUZZLING WINDOW

Tell your friend there is a window exactly five feet square. How can he make half the window space dark — and still have a square window five feet high and five feet wide? The illustration shows how.

THE BACKWARDS GAME

This one will keep your friend guessing for a while. Ask him to name a game in which the winning team always moves backwards. It's tug-of-war!

A KNOT—OR NOT?

Is this a knot? If you pulled the two loose ends until you had a straight piece of rope, would it have a knot?

ONE GOOD TURN—OR MORE

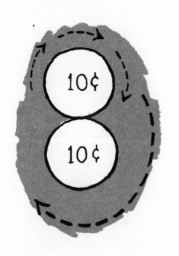

Place two identical coins on the table so they are touching each other. Now ask a friend if he can guess how many rotations the top coin will make as it moves around the other one during one complete revolution. What would you, yourself, guess?

PICTURE SECRET

Add and subtract the letters in the names of the things shown.

Clue: a very gentle creature.

Answers at back of the book.

LINE PUZZLERS

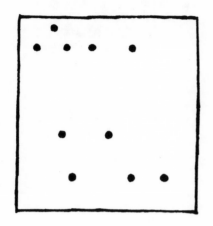

Copy the box and dots shown here, placing the dots exactly as shown. Then challenge someone to draw four straight lines, parallel to each other and at equal distances to each other, so that there will be exactly two dots in each section.

Oh, yes — you might try figuring it out, yourself, first!

Write the number 11030 on a piece of paper, as shown here. Then challenge a friend to make "a homeless man" out of this number, simply by adding two straight lines.

Remember that this is a trick . . . so there must be a trick answer!

This is an optical illusion. As you look at the diagonal lines, it doesn't seem possible that they are part of a straight line, but they are.

The reason this happens is that, as our eye follows the line upward, the parallel bars deflect our glance to the right, and so the next part of the line seems to have shifted to the right, also.

Answers at back of the book.

16

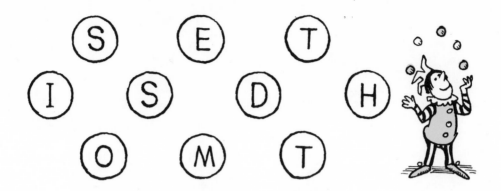

JUGGLE THE LETTERS

Take any of these letters and make up a one-letter word, then a two-letter word, then a three-letter word, and so on, up to a ten-letter word. You may only use the letters as often as they appear in the circles.

Write these letters on a sheet of paper. Then show them to a friend and ask him if he can make two different words out of them, each word using all the letters.

See if he can do it in less than a minute. See if you can!

There is a certain word that can be read forward and backward with these meanings. By reading the word forward, it means "exist." By reading it backward, it means "wicked."

Can you think of the word?

Answers at back of the book.

HALF A GLASS

Get a clear glass with vertical sides and fill it with water or a dark liquid. Then challenge someone to measure out exactly half the amount of liquid in the glass. Can it be done?

Yes! And here's how to do it: when you tip the glass as shown so that the line runs from one end of the bottom to the rim, you have exactly half a glass of liquid!

STOP AND GO

Here's a way to see air pressure at work. Punch a hole in the side of a can with a nail. When you let water run into the can, it will run out through the role. Now put a piece of cardboard on top of the can and press it down. The water will stop flowing because the air can no longer push down on the water!

TRICKS THAT DEFY GRAVITY!

You announce to your friends that you can pick up a pop bottle without so much as touching it with your hand or using any implement of metal, wood or cardboard. Offer to let anyone try.

When everyone has given up, bend an ordinary drinking straw near the bottom of it, insert it into the bottle as shown, and you'll be able to pick it up!

Here's a way to lift a glass as if by magic. Get a glass with a concave bottom and place it on a table, bottom up. Wet the palm of your hand and press it down on the glass. When you raise your hand slowly, you will lift the glass!

Give someone a glass jar and a marble, and then challenge him to hold it upside-down without having the marble fall out.

It can be done by causing the marble to whirl around inside the jar. Then raise the jar slowly as the marble whirls around until you have it upside-down. The marble won't fall out, because centrifugal force (the same force that keeps satellites in orbit) will keep it against the sides of the jar!

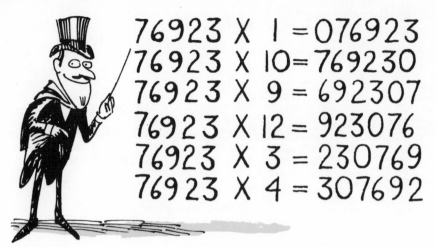

$$76923 \times 1 = 076923$$
$$76923 \times 10 = 769230$$
$$76923 \times 9 = 692307$$
$$76923 \times 12 = 923076$$
$$76923 \times 3 = 230769$$
$$76923 \times 4 = 307692$$

A MAGIC NUMBER

Here's an amazing trick to do with the number 76923. Multiply it by 1, 10, 9, 12, 3 and 4. If the products are listed as shown, every row of numbers across and every column of digits will add to the sum of 27.

Moreover, the digits fall in the same sequence when you read them down or across!

Now multiply 76923 by 2, 7, 5, 11, 6 and 8 . . . and you will get another surprise!

FIND THE NUMBER

See if you can find this number. When you add eight to it, then subtract eight from the sum, then multiply the remainder by eight, and then divide the product by eight, you get four. What is the number?

Check your answer with that given at the back of this book.

SUPER MAGIC SQUARE

This is one of the most amazing "magic squares" ever put together.

Add the numbers you see on any line, across, vertically or diagonally, and the answer is 264.

Now turn the page upside-down — and you still get the same answers!

96	11	89	68
88	69	91	16
61	86	18	99
19	98	66	81

THE 17 PUZZLE

Draw a triangle, as shown, and challenge someone to arrange the digits from 1 to 9 along the sides of it so that they add up to 17 along each side.

Can you do it? If you can't, or you want to check your answer, the solution is given at the back of the book.

BIRD IN A CAGE

There's a canary in a cage. The cage weighs five pounds and the bird weighs three ounces. How much do they both weigh together when the bird flies around inside the cage?

If you are "up in the air" for an answer, turn to the back of the book.

HOW MANY POTATOES?

Here's a way to fool your friend. Say to him, "Two men had a potato-peeling contest. The first man peeled two hundred and thirty-six potatoes; the second man peeled two hundred and won. How many potatoes did both peel together?" He'll say 437. But the answer is 436, because you said, "and won," not "and one."

TWO CHECKER PUZZLES

Place twelve checkers on a table (coins or counters may be substituted for the checkers, if you wish) and present this problem to a friend who likes puzzles. He is to arrange them to form six rows of four checkers each.

It's not easy to think of a solution, but there is one, and it may be found at the back of this book.

Get out the checker board and eight checkers. Challenge your friend to place the eight checkers on the board, each one on a different square, so that no two checkers are in the same horizontal line, no two are in the same vertical line, and no two are in the same diagonal line.

Turn to the back of this book for the answer.

LUTORGAP

NEDACIL

WESNED

NIPSA

LAITY

ACDEORU

Copy each set of letters shown and have your friends try to rearrange each group to spell the name of a country. The one who gets all six right first wins.

Where would you find these three peculiar things? In a zoo! They're actually the names of animals with the letters mixed up. Can you arrange them to get the names?

GROALTAIL

CORNCOA

FEGFAIR

lonesagi

ninege

wowdin

Here are three things you'll find in an automobile. Don't you recognize them? Just rearrange the letters in each word.

Answers at back of the book.

You have probably seen a United States dollar bill many times. So have your friends. Yet not many people can tell you how many times the word "one" and the numeral "1" appear on it. Do you know . . . or can you guess?

(Any 1's appearing in the serial number of the bill, of course, do not count.)

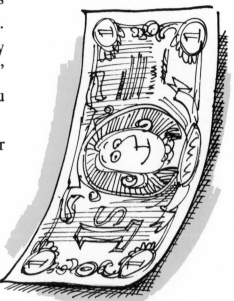

Try this one on a friend. Say, "I have two coins that total 35 cents, yet one is not a dime." Ask if he can explain that.

There is an explanation — but a tricky one.

If you have twenty coins worth $1.35, and the coins are all nickels and dimes — how many do you have of each kind of coin?

Answers at back of the book.

DIME WILL TELL

Ask your friend to hold a dime in one closed fist and a cent in the other one. He does this while you are not looking. Then ask him to multiply the value of the coin in his right hand by six (or any even number), multiply the value of the other coin by three (or any odd number), and add the results. If the number he gives you is even, the right hand holds the cent. If odd, the right hand has the dime.

YOUR AGE IS —

Here's a way to tell your friend's age, provided he is over ten years old. Tell him to add 90 to his age, cross off the first digit of the result, then add that digit to the remaining two digits.

When he tells you the answer, you simply add nine to it — and that's his age!

26

PUZZLING PLACES

No, these are not business trade-marks.
Each one is the name of a country or state.
Can you "decode" each one and say what
the place is?

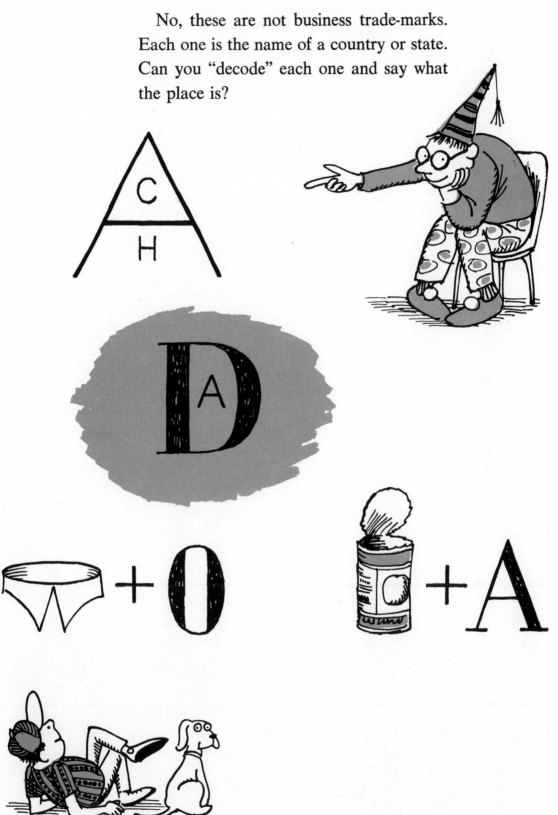

Answers at back of the book.

A PUT-TOGETHER PUZZLE

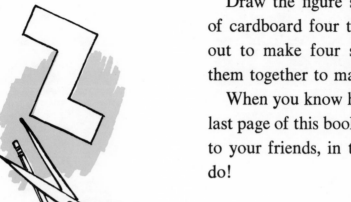

Draw the figure shown here on a piece of cardboard four times and cut each one out to make four such figures. Now put them together to make a cross.

When you know how (it is shown on the last page of this book), give the four shapes to your friends, in turn, and see how they do!

PLAY DETECTIVE

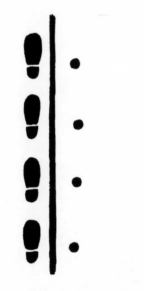

Suppose you were a detective and you found these tracks on some damp ground — would you be able to figure out how they were made and by whom?

To make sure, check the answer at the back of the book.

BLOW THE BOOK DOWN!

Stand a good-sized book upright on the edge of a table and challenge your friend to blow it down. When he gives up, just place the book on the closed end of a paper bag, blow into the open end — and you should be able to blow the book down.

HOW CAN THIS BE?

Two boys were born on the same day, at the same address, and with the same last name. Their parents were also the same — yet they were not twins. How can this be?

See the back of the book for the answer.

FIND THE SENTENCE

There is a sentence hidden in this square of letters. To find it, start with the letter Y and draw a continuous line from letter to letter. You can go to the left or right, up or down, but not diagonally. By the time you have gone through every letter, you should have a sentence.

The answer, if you don't find it, yourself, is given at the back of the book.

E	C	Y	F	O
E	N	O	U	U
T	E	D	D	N
N	N	D	T	H
E	S	I	H	E

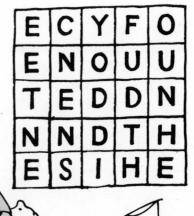

SEVEN IS THE NUMBER

Ask your friend to think of any number and add the next higher number to it in his mind. Tell him to add 13 to that result. Next, he divides by two. Finally, he subtracts the original number he thought of.

When he had done all this, you are able to tell him the original number he thought of. It's seven!

THAT'S ODD!

As a follow-up trick to the one just given, you can say to your friend, "Seven is an odd number. How can you make seven even?"

He will probably think of the number seven and thereby arrive at no solution. But you can make the word "seven" even by simply removing the "s"!

APPLES AND ORANGES

This should be an easy problem for you. If three apples are worth two oranges, how many oranges are 24 apples worth?

See the back of the book for the answer.

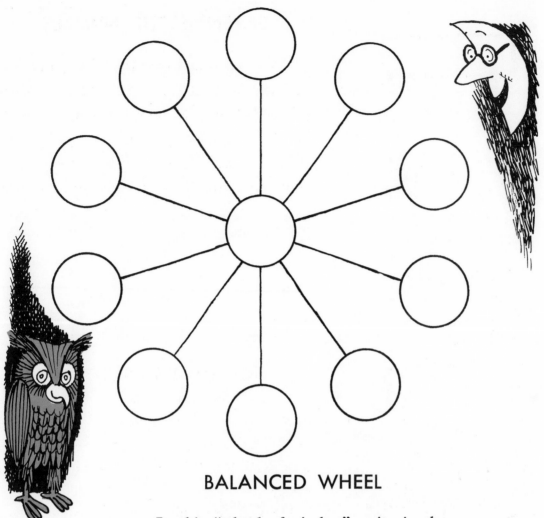

BALANCED WHEEL

In this "wheel of circles," write in the digits from 1 to 11, arranging them in the circles so that they add to the same amount in a straight line and in all directions. (There are three circles on the same straight line.)

DIGIT DEXTERITY

Write down the numbers 1 to 9 and give your friend this problem (after you try to solve it yourself): he is to use all the numbers, each only once, and put them down in such a way that they add to 99,999.

Answers at back of the book.

MAKE IT NINE

Arrange six matchsticks or toothpicks as shown and present this puzzle to someone: he must add five more (matchsticks or toothpicks) and make nine.

MAKE IT A HUNDRED

Arrange fifteen matches or toothpicks as shown. Now challenge your friend to remove six matches and leave a hundred.

MAKE IT RIGHT!

Arrange matches or toothpicks as shown and point out to your friend that one minus three does not really equal two. In other words, the equation is wrong, or false.

Now challenge him to make a correct equation by changing the position on only one match. It can be done!

Answers at back of the book.

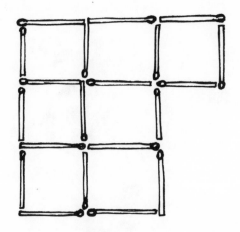

MIXED MATCHES

Arrange twenty matches to form seven squares, as shown in the illustration.

It is possible to rearrange only three matches and leave five squares. Can you do it?

Arrange twenty-four matches to form nine squares, as shown in the illustration.

The problem here is to remove eight matches and leave two squares. Can you do it?

Answers at back of the book.

FARM FOOLERS

1. The Haystacks

This is a tricky one. Say to your friend, "If a farmer had eight haystacks in one corner of a field, ten haystacks in another, seventeen in another, and six in the last, how many haystacks would there be altogether?"

What is your answer?

2. Cows and Chickens

A farmer decided to count his cows and chickens. But he did this by counting legs and heads. He counted 35 heads and 78 legs. How many cows and chickens did he have?

Answers at back of the book.

3. Eggs for Breakfast

There was a farmer named Jones who ate eggs for breakfast every day. But Farmer Jones didn't own any chickens, and he never got any eggs from chickens owned by anyone else. Where did Farmer Jones get his eggs?

4. A Woolly Problem

When Farmer Jones died, he left his two sons a flock of sheep to be divided equally. But the brothers agreed that one should take 20 sheep and the other 30. If the second brother paid the first brother $150, how much was each sheep worth?

Answers at back of the book.

Here is something about numbers that seems quite surprising. Select any number between 10 and 1,000. Add the digits in the number. Subtract the result from the number itself. Add the digits in the new number. The answer will always be either 9 or 18!

This is a tricky one. Can you write 24 with three equal digits? But none of the digits can be 8.

If you add a certain number to 3, the result is MORE than that number multiplied by 3. What is the number?

Answers at back of the book.

It's easy to think of four numbers that add up to 94. But can you think of four CONSECUTIVE numbers that total 94?

IMPOSSIBLE ARITHMETIC

Try this one on your friend. Ask him, "What number becomes nothing by adding one?"

See how this impossible arithmetic becomes possible at the end of the book.

MOVE-A-NUMBER

This should be easy. The problem is to move just one number from one of the columns into another column so that all columns add up to the same amount.

The way to do it is shown on the last page.

A	B	C
1	4	7
2	5	8
3	6	9
6	15	24

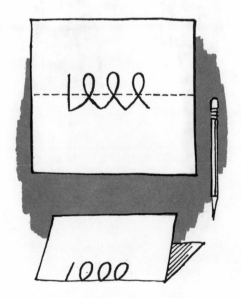

A TRICKY THOUSAND

It is possible to write the number 1000 without lifting the pencil from the paper. Each numeral is separate.

It doesn't seem possible, but here's the trick: fold the bottom third of the paper over. Then, where the edge meets the paper, draw what is shown here. When you lift the folded section, the separate numerals 1000 will be seen.

PEANUTS PUZZLE

A boy ate a hundred peanuts in five days. Each day he ate six more than on the previous day. How many did he eat on each of the five days?

THE BRUSH-OFF

Put a coin in the center of your palm. Give your friend a brush and bet him he can't brush the coin from your palm. He must use only the bristles of the brush and hold the brush level at all times. He won't be able to brush off the coin!

Answers at back of the book.

THE RISING TIDE

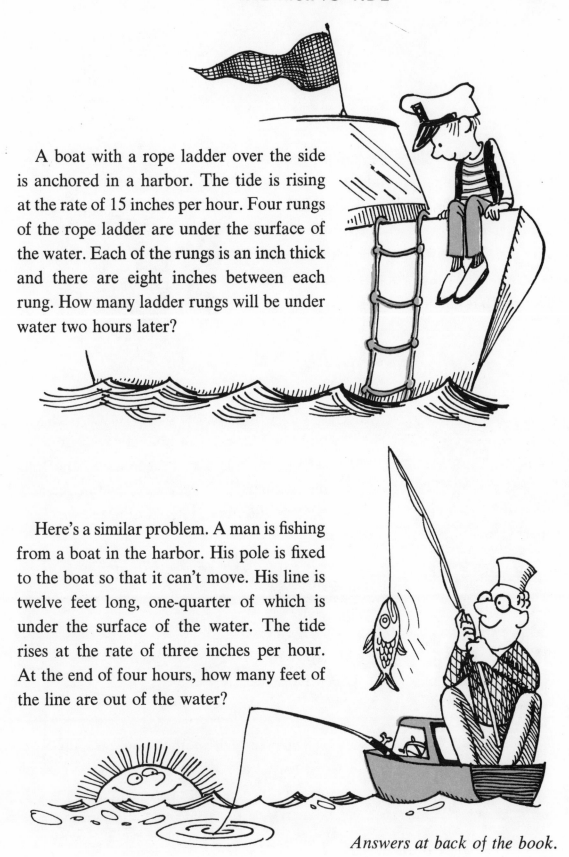

A boat with a rope ladder over the side is anchored in a harbor. The tide is rising at the rate of 15 inches per hour. Four rungs of the rope ladder are under the surface of the water. Each of the rungs is an inch thick and there are eight inches between each rung. How many ladder rungs will be under water two hours later?

Here's a similar problem. A man is fishing from a boat in the harbor. His pole is fixed to the boat so that it can't move. His line is twelve feet long, one-quarter of which is under the surface of the water. The tide rises at the rate of three inches per hour. At the end of four hours, how many feet of the line are out of the water?

Answers at back of the book.

Put a book on the table. Challenge your friend to place a pencil under the book without touching the book or the pencil. The trick is to have the pencil on a sheet of paper alongside. Pick up the paper with the pencil on it and place them both under the table. The pencil is under the book!

Put a dime in the center of an ordinary plate or saucer. Now challenge someone to take the coin out without touching the coin or the plate. The trick is to bend over and BLOW the dime out!

Tell your friend that you can stand on one corner of a newspaper and he can stand on the other, and he won't be able to touch you. Here's the trick: put the paper under a door and close it!

At a gathering of friends, announce confidently, "I bet I can put myself through a keyhole." You can be fairly sure someone will "take you up" on that!

Whereupon you simply write the word MYSELF on a piece of paper and push it through a keyhole!

Try this on your friend. Say, "I'll bet that if you clasp your hands the way I tell you, you won't be able to leave the room without unclasping them."

The trick is to make him clasp his hands around the leg of a heavy table!

Bet a friend you can make a pencil write any color you wish. When he says, "Show me!" simply write the name of the color your friend desires!

Here's an interesting experiment you can do that concerns your vision. Hold out two pencils at arm's length and make the tips touch. That's easy. Now close one eye and try to do it. It's not so easy.

The explanation for the difficulty is that our two eyes see an object from slightly different angles, and this helps us "position" it in space.

Ask your friend to lean against a wall so that his right shoe is against the wall, and his right leg and arm touch the wall. Then direct him to lift his left leg and keep it up without falling over. He won't be able to do it!

Tell your friend to stand with his heels against the wall. Put a coin at his feet. Now challenge him to pick up the coin without moving his feet or bending his knees. He won't be able to do it!

Bet your friend that he can't see his own eyeball move. If he stands in front of a mirror and tries it, he will see that it can't be done!

Place an ordinary ping-pong ball within a funnel large enough to hold it. Point the large end of the funnel upward and ask someone to try to blow the ball out. He won't be able to do it!

Tell your friend to sit back against a regular chair with his back straight against the chair. His feet must be flat on the floor and his arms folded across his chest.

Now ask him to rise from the chair in that position. He won't be able to do it.

THREE POSERS

Play detective and see if you can solve this puzzle:

A man who was served a cup of coffee in a restaurant called the waiter back to the table. Pointing to the cup, he said, "There seems to be a fly in my coffee. Please take this cup away and bring me a fresh cup of coffee."

The waiter promptly apologized, picked up the cup of coffee and took it away. He returned with a cup of coffee that had no fly in it. But when the customer tasted the coffee, he declared, "This is the same cup of coffee I had before!"

How did he know?

A medieval magician, carrying a bottle of liquid, approached the throne of his king.

"Sire," the magician said to the monarch, "I have here a most magic liquid. Such is its power that it will dissolve anything it touches."

"Anything?" asked the king.

"Anything!" replied the magician.

But the king knew that the magician was mistaken. How did he know?

A cannon ball is dropped from the top of a tower 250 feet high. At the same instant, another cannon ball of the same size and weight is fired horizontally (straight out) from a cannon.

Which cannon ball will reach the ground first?

Answers at back of the book.

SCRAMBLED NAMES

To look at these names, you might never think that they were three great men who were leaders of the fight for American independence.

Of course, the letters have been rearranged in each case. What you will have to do is to bring the letters into their original order to find out who these outstanding men were.

FNIRKNAL
FRONEFESJ
GNOTWINHAS

SONBIL
VENAGE
SLURSEBS

These are the names of three cities in Europe. No, not the way they are shown here —the letters have been rearranged in each case.

To find out what the cities are, bring the letters into their original order.

Three important professions are indicated by the names shown here, though the letters have been rearranged in each case.

To find out what the professions are, bring the letters into their original order.

CRATEHE
WAYREL
ISTENCTIS

HOW MANY?

In all of these puzzles, use the letters given in any order, but only as often as they appear in the boxes.

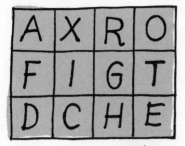

How many names of animals can you make from the letters in these boxes? See if you can form at least ten of them.

How many words about parts of the human body can you make from the letters in these boxes? See if you can form at least nine of them.

The letters in these boxes will also make words about parts of the human body. See if you can form at least ten of them.

Answers at back of the book.

CHANGE THE WORD

In these three puzzles, see if you can change the first word to the last one by changing only one letter in the word with each move. For example, you could change BOAT into CASH as follows: (BOAT, COAT, COST, CAST, CASH.) Use the boxes, writing in the words from top to bottom.

Answers at back of the book.

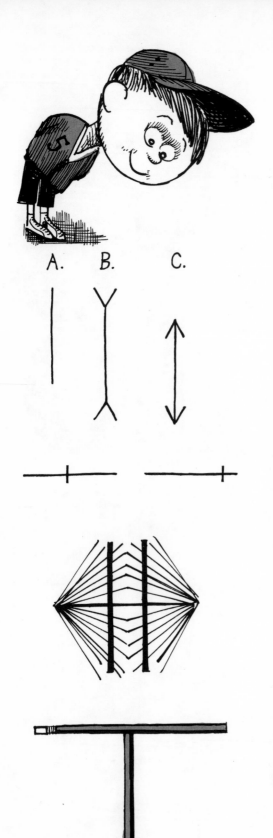

EYE FOOLERS

Here are some examples of how your own eyes can play tricks on you.

Which of the long lines shown in the figures marked A, B and C is the longest?

Most people would probably guess "B," but measurement will show that it is really "C."

Now ask someone to guess which of the two lines shown here is longer.

The truth is, they're equal in length. The right one seems longer because the vertical line pulls the eye beyond the end of the line.

Look at this illustration carefully. Are the two dark lines parallel (even with each other) or are they bent inward?

The lines are really not bent, but they appear to be that way because of the angles formed by the lighter lines.

Take two unsharpened pencils exactly the same size and set them in the form of a "T," as shown in the picture. Do this before you have a friend look at the formation. Then have him tell you which pencil is the longer one.

Most people will guess that the pencil forming the downstroke of the "T" is the longer one. Place the pencils side by side to show how wrong a guess can be.

CALENDAR CALCULATIONS

Don't throw away your old monthly calendar sheets—use them to show your friends this baffling trick:

Ask a friend to form an outline with pencil or crayon around nine dates on the calendar, the only restriction being that this is done in the form of a three-by-three square with all dates (numbers) included. There must be no blank spaces. You don't see what dates he chooses.

Now ask him to tell you the smallest of these numbers, whereupon, within a few short seconds, you are able to give him the sum (total) of all nine numbers! An amazing feat! It will take your friend a much longer time to add the numbers together himself and admit that the total you gave him is indeed correct.

To be able to do this, all you need do is add eight to the number your friend gives you (the smallest number) and multiply the result by nine.

Here's a way to use your hands to tell you how many days there are in each month. Hold up your fists, as shown in the picture. Start from the left and call the first knuckle January. The space before the next knuckle is February. The next knuckle is March,

All months that fall on knuckles have 31 days. All months that fall in the spaces between the knuckles have 30 days. In the case of February, of course, there are only 28 days, except during a leap year, when there are 29.

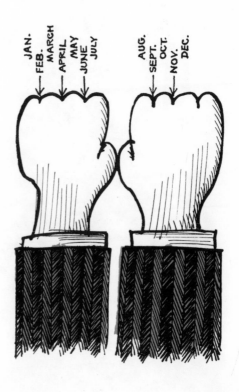

EGGS-TRAORDINARY EGGS-HIBITIONS

This is a trick—really a demonstration of air pressure—that never ceases to amuse and amaze people.

Use a hard-boiled egg with its shell peeled off and a bottle whose opening is somewhat smaller than the narrow diameter of the egg. If you wish, you may want to challenge your friend to make the egg go through the neck of the bottle—without eating any of it, of course!

How can it be done? Simply drop a lighted match—or a small piece of paper that you have ignited with the match—into the bottle and immediately place the egg atop the bottle. The egg will be sucked right into the bottle!

The scientific explanation is that the burning of the match or paper uses up most of the oxygen within the bottle and creates a partial vacuum which forces the egg (the pressure of the outside air "pushes") through the narrower opening and into the bottle.

Place a fresh egg in a glass of water. After it sinks to the bottom, challenge your friends to bring the egg to the top of the glass without touching it. Here's how to do it:

Hold the glass under a water faucet and gradually turn on the water. As the flow increases, the egg will rise to the surface and stay there.

Challenge your friends to make an egg spin. They won't be able to do it. Then you show them that you apparently have some mysterious power, because you can make an egg spin without a bit of trouble.

The trick is that you give your friends an uncooked (raw) egg to spin. When you try, you use a hard-boiled egg. A fresh egg won't spin, but a hard-boiled one will!

It is said—though it is probably no more than a story having little or no basis in fact —that Christopher Columbus once amazed some people by being able to stand an egg on end.

You can do as well as Columbus in this particular instance. Just shake the egg that you will use—this is all done beforehand—so that the yolk will break. You may have to shake rather vigorously. Allow the broken yolk to settle for a few minutes.

When you are ready to "outdo" Columbus, just make sure that you have a table with a cloth on it and that you balance the egg carefully. You will find that you can do this without too much difficulty. (That will be YOUR discovery!)

It is also possible to do the previous egg trick another way—without breaking the yolk. The trick is to put a small amount of salt on the white tablecloth, to form a tiny mound. When you place the egg carefully into the salt, it will balance.

In this method, it is possible to brush away the salt (without, of course, calling attention to it) in the act of picking up the egg and handing it to someone, as you ask him to try to duplicate your feat. He will naturally not be able to do it.

TWENTY-FIVE DOTS

Copy this square of twenty-five dots and challenge a friend to connect twelve of these dots with straight lines to make a perfect cross that will have five dots inside it and eight dots outside.

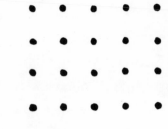

TEN DOTS

Can you draw four straight lines which will pass through every one of the dots shown here? You must not take your pencil off the paper!

Answers at back of the book.

FOUR DOTS

Copy the four dots exactly as shown. Then challenge someone to draw a square which has one of the four dots in each side.

THREE BREATHTAKING TRICKS

Hang two apples by means of string from a towel rack or any similar support. The apples themselves should hang about one inch apart.

If you or a friend will now blow between them—as hard as possible—you will discover that the force of breath alone won't blow them apart. Instead, it will cause the apples to bump together!

Take a small piece of paper, about one inch square, and roll it into a small tight ball.

Now lay a soda bottle on its side—it is empty, of course—and push the small paper pellet into the neck of the bottle, about an inch from the opening. (Use your finger, or a pencil.)

What do you suppose would happen if you blew into the bottle? Do you think the tiny paper ball would be blown into it?

Try it. When you blow into the bottle, the ball will come flying out!

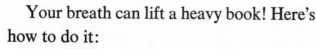

Your breath can lift a heavy book! Here's how to do it:

Put a large dictionary or heavy book directly on top of a hot-water bottle. When you hold the mouth of the bag tightly against your mouth and blow hard, the book will be raised quite easily.

Here's a trick to show that half of eleven equals six.

Arrange six matches to form the Roman figure eleven (XI), as shown. Now take away the bottom three matches—or half of eleven—and the Roman number VI remains!

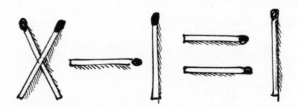

By arranging the matches as shown, an equation is formed in Roman numerals which reads ten minus one equals one. Obviously, this is not correct. How can you make it correct by merely changing the position of one match?

Answers at back of the book.

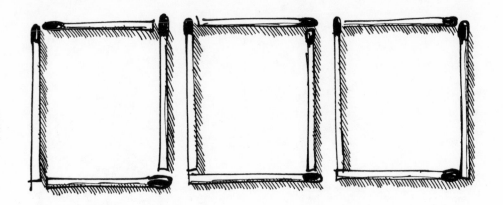

Arrange twelve matches to form three separate squares, as shown. Announce that you can take one match away and have one remain.

Impossible? No. Tricky? Yes.

Answers at back of the book.

Hand your friend five matches. Then give him six more. Ask him to count them. When he says "Eleven," you say that he is mistaken. "Five matches plus six matches make nine!"

To prove it, take the eleven matches and arrange them to spell out the word NINE, as shown.

A variation of the last trick is to lay nine matches on the table and state that you will make ten out of the nine matches without breaking any.

Naturally, the way to do it is to form the word TEN with the matches, as shown.

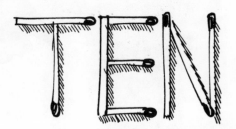

DIVIDE BY SEVEN

This is a tricky problem, but it can be solved. The baseball players appear to be perplexed—and well they might be. They have been asked to arrange themselves so that the number on their uniforms form one number that can be divided evenly by seven.

Can you help them? Remember, we said it was tricky.

Answers at back of the book.

PENS AND PIGS

This is another tricky problem, which is simply this: can you put nine pigs in four pens so that each of the four pens has an odd number of pigs?

WORD MAGIC

Hand your friend a pencil and a pad or sheet of paper. Ask him to write a sentence on it, but not to show it to you.

You then say, "I will write the same as you on my paper"—and proceed to write something which will presumably match whatever he writes.

When the time comes for you to show what you've written, you do so. On your paper is written, "The same as you." That is exactly what you said you would do!

Can you think of an English word of four letters which reads the same upside-down as it does right side up, when printed in capital letters?

The word is

Can you think of an English word of four letters meaning "water" which becomes a word meaning "land" by the change of one letter?

Here are the two words:

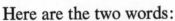

THE $700 MYSTERY

You may have to do a little thinking, and use pencil and paper, to solve this puzzle.

A man had $700. He divided it into quarters, half dollars and dollars so that there was an equal number of each. How many of each denomination did he divide it into?

Answers at back of the book.

THE DOLLAR MYSTERY

Have you ever examined a dollar bill closely? Do you remember what you saw on it?

See if you can answer this question: which way is Washington facing?

THREE FUNNY TRICKS

Here's a trick that's sure to fool your friend. Ask him to stand in front of you. Take a clothes brush and brush your own coat. At the same time, rub his coat lightly with the palm of your hand. When you ask him what you're doing, he's sure to say you're brushing HIS coat!

In this trick you announce, "I bet I can go out of the room on two legs and come back with six."

Someone is sure to want to see THAT! And what you do is simply pick up a chair in another room and bring it back with you!

Tell your friend, "I bet you can't take off your coat alone." As soon as he starts to take off his coat, though, you take your coat off, too!

A SECRET MESSAGE

Here's how to send a secret message. Dip a clean pen into vinegar and write the message on a sheet of heavy writing paper. Be sure to make a good heavy line as you write. This "ink" will soon dry and become invisible.

All your friend has to do to read the message is hold the paper an inch or two above a candle flame and move it back and forth slowly. The message will appear again!

THE MAGIC FLAME

Here's a way to light a candle without touching a flame to the wick of the candle.

First light a candle with a match. After it burns for a minute, blow it out. As soon as you blow it out, strike a match and hold it about an inch above the candlewick. The flame will actually jump down to the candle and light the wick.

The secret is to watch the curl of smoke that goes up from the candle after it has been put out. When the match meets this smoke, the flame shoots down to the candle.

THE UNDERWATER CANDLE

Here's how to make a candle burn below the surface of a glass of water.

Put a nail in the bottom of the candle so that the candle will float in a vertical position. Then light it. The melting wax will form a little well in which the wick will burn.

NAIL
IN
CANDLE

SHADOW OF A DIFFERENCE

Two identical planes are flying over a field. One plane is fifty feet above the field and the other is five hundred feet above the field. What will be the difference in the size of their shadows?

The answer is: "no difference." Since the size of a shadow depends on the distance from the light source, and the sun is 93,-000,000 miles away, the slight difference of 450 feet between the two planes isn't enough to make a perceptible difference.

THROUGH THE TABLE

Get a lump of wrapped sugar, secretly unwrap it very carefully, and take out the sugar. Then close the ends of the paper so it looks as if the sugar is still in it.

Have the sugar in your lap beforehand.

To present, show the empty packet and place it a short distance away from you and the edge of the table. Then bring your hand down on it hard so it flattens the paper. The sugar is gone!

Now reach under the table and get the lump of sugar. Bring it forth and toss it on the table. The illusion has been that the sugar penetrated both its own wrapper and the solid table.

THE THREE R'S

Using the same two letters to fill in the spaces on each line, can you complete these three words?

The answer may be found on page 76.

R _ _ _
_ R _ _
_ _ R

THE FOUR L'S

Draw the letter L, as shown, on a piece of paper. The problem is to cut or form four small L's within this area, all having the same basic shape as the large one you see.

The answer may be found on page 76.

CUTTING THE PIE

Next time Mother bakes a pie, try this on her. Ask her what would be the most pieces she can cut with four straight cuts.

Try to work it out, yourself.

The answer may be found on page 77.

SEA WORDS

This is a word-forming puzzle. You form a five-letter word by choosing its first letter from the first vertical column, its second letter from the second vertical column, and so on, until you have a five-letter word.

The puzzle-problem is to form five words in this manner, all five words relating to the sea.

```
L H O H R
Y T E L E
W C N A M
O A A R N
S I C E T
```

Answers at back of the book.

```
-LUM-
-XTR-
-EBE-
-LOR-
-LFI-
-OMI-
-ABL-
```

LETTER FILL

In each of the letter combinations shown here you can form a word by adding a letter to the beginning and the end. The trick is to form words so that the first letters and the last letters will also form words when you read them from top to bottom.

PICK UP THE ICE CUBE

Float an ice cube in a glass of water and challenge your friends to try to lift it out with a loop of string. They won't be able to do it.

Then you show them how easy it is. Wet the loop of string first, then lay it on the ice cube and sprinkle it with salt. After three minutes, lift the string and you will be able to lift out the ice cube.

A.   B.

PICK UP THE GLASS

Get a glass and a balloon. Challenge your friend to pick up the glass with the balloon—without touching the glass with his hands.

The way to do it—as you can demonstrate—is to hold the balloon inside the glass with the bottom part touching the bottom of the glass. Blow into the balloon, inflating it, close the top end—and you'll be able to lift the glass!

PICK UP THE DIME

Announce that you can pick up a dime from a table without touching the dime with any part of your body, and without using any metal, wood, or cardboard instrument.

The way to do it is to place the bottom opening of a drinking straw against the dime and suck up the air from the other end. You'll be able to pick up the dime.

THE VANISHING WATER

Cover a glass of water with a hat and say to your friend, "I bet I can drink all the water in that glass without touching the hat."

You really have to be tricky to do this. Take a pencil, put one end to your lips and the other end to the hat, and remark that it is a magic straw. Pretend that you are drinking the water, as you would an ice-cream soda. Then say, "All right — the water is gone."

When your friend lifts the hat to see if it's true, you simply pick up the glass and drink the water without ever touching the hat. (Your friend was the one who touched the hat when he lifted it up.)

THE WALKING DIME

Place a dime on a table that has a table-cloth. Then place a nickel on each side of the dime so that you can put a glass upside down on the two nickels, as shown in the picture.

Now challenge your friend to get the dime from under the glass without touching the glass, the dime, or the nickels.

The way to do it is to scratch the table-cloth with your fingernail as close to the glass as possible. Short fast scratches will soon cause the dime to "walk" out from under the glass.

HAVE A FEW FITS

Make this drawing on a large sheet of paper. Then cut the square into seven pieces along the lines shown. Mix up the pieces and challenge your friend to put them together so as to form a square. It won't be easy.

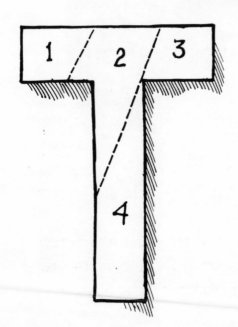

Copy this cross on a large sheet of paper. Cut it along the lines shown in the picture. Challenge your friend to put it together to make a cross. He'll find it harder than he thinks.

Copy the letter T, as shown, making it quite large. Draw the dotted lines, as shown, and cut it into four pieces along the dotted lines. Now challenge your friend to put the pieces together to make the letter T.

THE INVISIBLE THIMBLE

Here's a good joke to play on your friend. Tell him, "I bet I can put a thimble where everybody in the room can see it except you."

Then put the thimble on your friend's head.

THE IMPOSSIBLE FOLD

If you have a friend who thinks he's strong, give him a sheet of newspaper, two full pages. Challenge him to fold it eight times. He may think that there's nothing to it, but no matter how much he tries, he won't be able to fold it eight times.

The reason is that the paper would have 128 thicknesses on the eighth fold — and paper can't be folded that many times.

PENCIL DRAWINGS

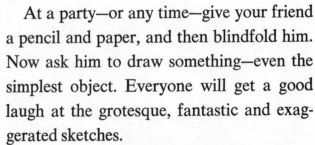

At a party—or any time—give your friend a pencil and paper, and then blindfold him. Now ask him to draw something—even the simplest object. Everyone will get a good laugh at the grotesque, fantastic and exaggerated sketches.

This can also be a test for your friends. Give them all a sheet of paper and a pencil and ask each one to draw a circle the size of a quarter, a line the length of a standard cigarette, and a rectangle the size of a postage stamp. When their drawings are compared with the actual things, it will be a surprise to everyone to discover the inaccuracies.

Draw an oblong box and challenge a friend to draw in the American flag from memory. You'll be surprised and amused to see how many mistakes he makes.

JOURNEY TO THE CENTER OF THE CIRCLE

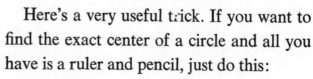

Here's a very useful trick. If you want to find the exact center of a circle and all you have is a ruler and pencil, just do this:

Tear off a corner of a sheet of paper. Place it on the circle, as shown in the picture. Where the sides of the paper touch the circle (A and B), make two marks. When you join them, you will have the diameter. And half that line will be the center of the circle.

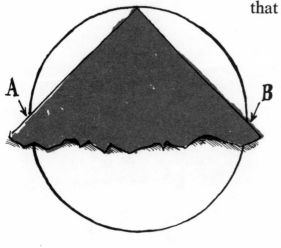

A STRAIGHT LINE

Tell your friends you can make a perfectly straight line across a table without using a ruler or any other object with a straight edge.

The trick is to take a long rubber band that has been cut, have the ends held for you, and then rub chalk along the band. Then ask your two friends to hold the rubber-band ends at opposite ends of the table. You take the center, stretch it up and let go. It will snap back and make a straight line on the table.

IT'S MAGNETISM!

Spill a little salt on a bare table. Now challenge someone to remove it—but without touching the table or the salt, and without blowing or fanning of any kind.

The trick is to rub an ordinary plastic comb on your sleeve several times and bring it near the salt. The salt will seem to jump to the comb.

You can make a playing card stick to a smooth wall without using paste, glue, tape or any adhesive, and without nails or tacks. It is done—preferably on a dry day—by shuffling your feet on the rug or carpet while holding the card in your hand. Then slam the card onto the wall. In cold weather, static electricity will cause the card to stick to the wall.

Tear a piece of paper into small scraps and place them on a table. Announce that you can "magnetize" a pencil so it will cause those papers to move. Rub the pencil on your sleeve, and as you bring it close to the paper, blow gently. The papers will move away as if the pencil is causing this movement. Be sure that no one sees you blowing.

A DELICATE BALANCE

This is a trick to make your friends think you can balance a glass on the edge of a plate, as shown in the first picture.

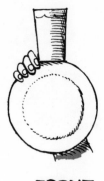

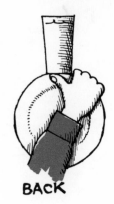

FRONT   BACK

Here's what you do. As you put the glass (which may contain liquid) on top of the plate, raise your thumb behind it to hold the glass in place, as shown in the second picture.

SIX GLASSES

Arrange six glasses in a row, three of them filled with water or some other liquid, as shown.

The problem, you tell a friend, is to arrange the glasses so that they stand one filled, one empty, one filled, one empty, one filled, one empty. This must be done by moving or touching only one glass.

The way to do it is to take glass No. 4 and pour the water into glass No. 1, then replace glass No. 4.

THE FIREPROOF CUP

Did you know that you can hold a paper cup over a gas flame without having the paper cup catch fire?

The trick is to fill the cup with cold water. The heat will be conducted away by the cold water.

IT MAKES CENTS

Put four 1¢ pieces on the table and challenge someone to arrange them so that there are two straight lines with three cents in each line.

The trick is to lay out three of the 1¢ pieces in the form of a triangle, and then put the fourth cent on top of the others.

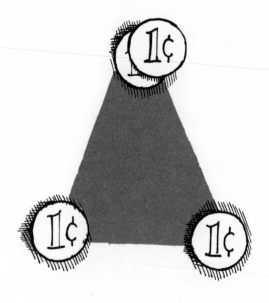

FIGURE IT OUT!

Can you figure out this number? It consists of two digits. If you multiply the digits and multiply the result by two, you get the actual number.

18
24 ? 32
14 : 46
98

Answers at back of the book.

A ONE-LINER

Look at this drawing carefully and then try to draw it with one continuous line. Do not cross any lines or go over any lines twice.

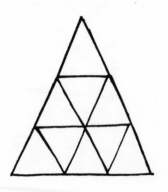

THREE "HANDY" TRICKS

Tell your friend to put his hand flat on a table, with his middle finger under his hand, as shown in the picture. Now challenge him to lift his third finger without moving his middle finger. He won't be able to do it!

Here's a way to prove your friends don't know how to count!

Tell someone to cross his middle and index fingers and then close his eyes. Hold out your hand with two marbles in it. Ask him to touch the marbles with the tips of his crossed fingers and tell you how many there are. He's sure to say there are three or even four. His crossed fingers will fool him!

Ask your friend to stand with her back to you with her arms out. Now tell her to keep her arms straight and you take each of her wrists and pull her arms backward slowly. Make the backs of her hands touch.

When you do this, she simply won't believe that the backs of her hands were touching. It's a trick the senses play on us.

ANSWERS

How Many? (Pages 8-9)

CLOTHING: Hat, tie, cap, coat, shoe, suit, vest, shirt, skirt, sock, pants, strap, scarf, jacket, hose.

INSECTS: Ant, moth, gnat, mite, fly, flea, lice, wing, pest, wasp.

EATING: Dine, dish, fish, fed, sup, pie, ate, bread, bite, bun, chew, soup, peas, cup, tea, bone, sip.

CIRCUS: Tent, clown, ring, lion, tiger, cage, acrobat, giant, seal, beast, dogs, band, dancer.

FARM ANIMALS: Goats, fox, hens, frog, colt, owl, wren, nest, swan, crow, dog, hog, cat, loon, goose.

BIRDS: Wren, nest, wing, egg, eagle, swan, cage, crane, crow, beak, hawk, owl.

Change the Word (Pages 12-13)

STAR, SEAR, SEAT, FEAT, FEET; SNOW, SLOW, FLOW, FLAW, FLAG; GIFT, LIFT, LIFE, LIKE, LAKE; FARM, HARM, HARE, HIRE, HIVE; PIPE, PILE, PALE, SALE, SALT; BOAT, COAT, COST, CAST, CASH.

A Knot — or Not? (Page 15)

No knot.

One Good Turn — or More (Page 15)

The coin will make exactly two revolutions.

Picture Secret (Page 15)

Lamb.

Line Puzzlers (Page 16)

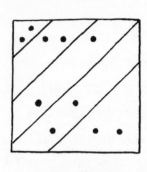

HOBO

Juggle the Letters (Page 17)

There are many solutions possible, but one of them would be: I, do, met, shot, timed, desist, methods, moistest, Methodist, Methodists.

The words are "unite" and "untie."

The word is LIVE.

Find the Number (Page 20)

The number is four. (All of the arithmetical steps simply cancel out each other.)

The 17 Puzzle (Page 21)

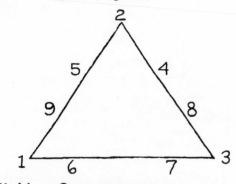

Bird in a Cage (Page 22)

Five pounds. The flapping of the bird's wings pushes the air down and it is driven out of the cage and displaced outside. If the bird were in a sealed cage or box, the weight would be five pounds and three ounces.

Two Checker Puzzles (Page 23)

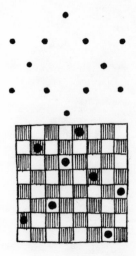

Scrambled Letters (Page 24)

Portugal, Iceland, Sweden, Spain, Italy, Ecuador.

Alligator, raccoon, giraffe.

Gasoline, engine, window.

Money Mysteries (Page 25)

"One" and "1" appear sixteen times.

Just say, "One is a quarter, the OTHER is a dime."

Thirteen nickels and seven dimes.

Puzzling Places (Page 27)

China (C, H in A); India (in D, A); Colorado (collar, add O); Canada (can, add A).

A Put-Together Puzzle (Page 28)

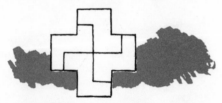

Play Detective (Page 28)

The tracks were made by a man with a wooden leg, pushing a wheelbarrow.

How Can This Be? (Page 29)

They were two of a set of triplets.

Find the Hidden Sentence (Page 29)

"You found the hidden sentence."

Apples and Oranges (Page 30)

Sixteen oranges.

Balanced Wheel (Page 31)

Digit Dexterity (Page 31)

$$\begin{array}{r} 98765 \\ +\ 1234 \\ \hline 99999 \end{array}$$

Make it Nine (Page 32)

NINE

Make it a Hundred (Page 32)

Make it Right! (Page 32)

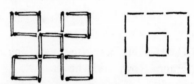

Mixed Matches (Page 33)

Farm Foolers (Pages 34-35)

1. When you put the haystacks "all together," this makes only one haystack!

2. 31 chickens, 4 cows.

3. From ducks. They were duck eggs!

4. $30 each.

Numbers, Please (Page 36)

$22 + 2 = 24$.

One.

22, 23, 34, 25.

Impossible Arithmetic (Page 37)

N plus ONE equals NONE. The "one" you add is one letter.

Move-a-Number (Page 37)

Move the "9" from the C-column to the A-column.

Peanuts Puzzle (Page 38)

8, 14, 20, 26 and 32.

The Rising Tide (Page 39)

Four rungs. As the tide rises, the boat will rise with it, and since the ladder is attached to the boat, it will rise, too!

Nine feet. Again, as the tide rises, the boat and everything on it rises, too!

Three Posers
(Page 44)

(1) The man knew it was the same cup of coffee because he had put sugar in the coffee before he found the fly in it.

(2) The king knew the magician was mistaken, because if the liquid dissolved everything it touched, it would dissolve the bottle, too.

(3) Both cannon balls will reach the ground at the same time. Gravity acts on each one in the same way, so each one will approach the ground at the same rate.

Scrambled Names
(Page 45)

(1) Franklin, Jefferson, Washington.
(2) Lisbon, Geneva, Brussels.
(3) Teacher, Lawyer, Scientist.

How Many?
(Page 46)

ANIMALS: Dog, hog, doe, goat, cat, toad, fox, frog, rat, tiger.

HUMAN BODY (1): Arm, ear, nail, chin, neck, hand, hair, ankle, lip.

HUMAN BODY (2): Ear, face, arm, toe, foot, nail, lip, nose, hair, rib, chest, bone, chin.

Change the Word
(Page 47)

LAST, PAST, PART, PERT, PERK
CLAN, PLAN, PLAY, PRAY, PREY
NEST, PEST, POST, PORT, PORK

Twenty-Five Dots
(Page 52)

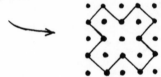

Ten Dots
(Page 52)

Four Dots
(Page 52)

Matching Numbers
(Pages 54-55)

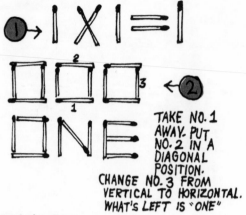

TAKE NO. 1 AWAY. PUT NO. 2 IN A DIAGONAL POSITION. CHANGE NO. 3 FROM VERTICAL TO HORIZONTAL. WHAT'S LEFT IS "ONE"

Divide by Seven
(Page 56)

One of the players stands on his head, and the three players form the number 931.

Pens and Pigs
(Page 56)

First make one large pen, and then make three small pens inside it. Put three pigs in each of the small pens, and the large pen will have nine pigs!

The $700 Mystery
(Page 58)

Four hundred of each.

The Dollar Mystery
(Page 58)

George Washington faces to the right on a dollar bill.

The Three R's
(Page 62)

Rat, art, tar.

The Four L's
(Page 62)

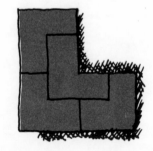

Cutting the Pie
(Page 62)

Sea Words
(Page 63)
    Liner, yacht, whale, storm, ocean.

Letter Fill
(Page 63)
    Plumb, extra, rebel, flora, elfin, comic, table.
The vertical words read "perfect balance."

Figure it Out!
(Page 72)
    36.

A One-Liner
(Page 72)

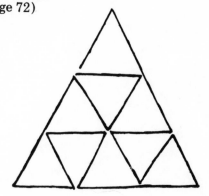

QUIZEROO

john huehnergarth